I Saw Michael Caine

James A. Smith

William Cornelius Harris Publishing

In collaboration

With

London Poetry Books

ISBN 978-1-911232-50-6

William Young

34 Birchwood Close, Bordesley Road SM4 5NH

W
C
H
P

London Poetry Books

With grateful thanks to
Bryan Bass,
the English teacher who saw some potential blossoms
in the waste ground of my education.

Contents

Three at Random

Three Dreamscapes

Love Pavement

Midday sun on Love Pavement...
Here he comes, singing,
the whites of his eyes pink to the dust.
Smoke, refusing to wreathe about his head,
settles in abstract grey fragments in the warm, still air.

"In the middle of the street, they lovey-dovey,
but I'm all alone,
walking on the stones,
of Love Pavement."

He has a casual, velvet voice.
Hear him sing Sinatra in the shower.
With all the hissing and steaming,
it's like an original 78.

"Lookin' for my baby in the gutter,
when she left I heard her mutter 'Love Pavement.'"

I purchase an ice cream with a bank-note I dreamed up.
The vendor holds it to the light, then exclaims:
"Hey, it's only play money,
look at the picture."
I grab the ice cream and run,
past blighted staircases,
uncles with bad feet,
renegade MPs,
documentary teams.
The BBC retreats on Love Pavement.

Room above the pavement,
small boxes, empty cups,

slices of conversation on cheap china dishes,
eaten with a gentleman's relish.
Relics of amours, a postcard of the Berlin Wall.
The man in the suit is the suit more than the man.
He talks in threads;
he carries a gun to protect the suit.
The woman facing him loves suits,
and she's quite fond of the man.
She notices that his socks match his suit.
Last week they clashed.
He's learning…

*"Makin' hay from the weeds between the slabs, yeah,
lost my baby that way, yeah,
see how that grabs ya,
down on Love Pavement."*

Another room, just above the corner.
White, everything is white.
The gentleman inside is white,
almost invisible in his chair.
He explores the Arctic walls
with their insinuated snow-scapes.
A slender tube of milk rests, cow content, by his elbow.
He likes things to be clean, he prefers virgins.

Suppose there is a horse trough beneath a yew tree,
an obsolete stone basin,
dedicated to a forgotten memory.
The singer sings right up close,
crooning into the tap like it's a microphone.
Suppose I am standing in the deeper shadows,
watching and listening with freshly acquired inscrutability.

8

"In the street they lovey-dovey sure,
just like before,
before my girl made a statement,
said that she was going down to Loooovvveee Pavement."

I fictionalise the singer's past.
I give him snakes as pets, and monstrous parentage.
I give him ancestors he could never envision.
I give him my small change.

A girl leans against the railings,
she's bored,
she came to Love Pavement for entertainment.
More eyes than she can see or count take in her denim and trainers,
but nobody feels any lust, nobody passes her by with a backward
glance.
She lights a cigarette to pass the time.

The man in white yawns, mouth agape to reveal
sparkling ivory teeth.
His sheets gaze at him, enticingly.
They murmur post-prandial lullabies into the spotless air.

"I was discussing my fate,
feeling no hate,
had my life on a plate,
right here on the pavement."

I pace up and down,
eyeing the promenaders,
feeling strangely self-conscious,
like a schoolboy outside a porn cinema.
Horizons rest, no beckoning, no threat,
tactfully static and carefully geometric.

9

Here on the pavement pity flows
like bitter aloes from the end of a child's chewed pencil.
"Don't do that, you'll make your gums bleed."
"Oh mum, I'm not, I was only mouthing it,
I was only thinking…"
"You're old enough to stop that sort of thing."
"Sorr-rreee!"

*"Baby can you read my mind,
can't remember the last time I dined,
you were my food and drink,
you left me on the brink,
crawling to the kerb,
ooh ooh, Love Pavement."*

I walk across the street,
and take in the view,
don't know what to do,
stand by a chatter of boys,
emphasising every curl of their lips;
then I slip a gear, watch the girl,
watch a flag unfurl,
flopping in the breeze,
forty feet or more above Love Pavement.

The gentleman in white draws back his snowdrift curtains,
peers frostily into the street,
winces at the singing, shambling figure beneath his window.
He dabs at a shadow,
hoping to erase it with his obsession.
A dog licks up drops of molten vanilla ice cream,
the pale gent approves.
The reason? The dog, like the ice cream,
is white.

I hide from the ice man's gaze,
invisible again behind the yew tree.
I wait for time to kill,
I wait for time to stand still.

"I'm gonna take a walk,
shuffle words like Brando talk,
get down to the basement,
down there where my baby lives,
no one receives, everyone gives,
down below Love Pavement."

The singer's voice conjures
Raymond Chandler
channelling Philip Marlowe
in a cool, twilit, sun-excluded bar,
at the perfect time of day for a Gimlet
with Rose's Lime Juice
to sweat quietly on the counter before him,
awaiting the first ecstatic sip.

On the corner a cigarette is ground into the ground,
a heel turns, and with a well-rehearsed flick of the hip,
the girl has gone.

The setting sun is now bisected by an aerial,
beneath the aerial is a television.
Upon the television a silent moving picture is watched
by sightless eyes.
Annie of the cluttered room wanted romance,
her china has roses on the rim,
she keeps every love letter in an inlaid box.
In this box they are laid.

The man in the suit closes the door upon his lady-friend,
wipes the handle, and his hands
carefully on a large pocket-handkerchief,
steps onto the street, and then holds forth,
speaking clearly into a small Dictaphone.

"Behavioural patterns observed to be perfectly in keeping
with the classless buildings.
Analyse,
break down into basic meaning, each statement that she made.
Now stripped and reduced to a nugget of unfortunate truth,
to justify the reason and method of my departure."

He lowers the device,
pauses, and then resumes with gloating finality;

"Nobody tells me that my clothes
know more about life than I do."

Love Pavement – slight return no.1

Gawky girl holds a midnight blue dress against herself
and becomes instantly beautiful
Afternoon sun on Love Pavement
Passers-by pass by and others pause here under the cool awning
where the cigar smoke coils
on Love Pavement

You stroke your nose,
lost in a sensual moment
and then your friend arrives
and you are faintly disturbed that she saw you first
sitting outside the Cat in the Grapevine Cafe
dreaming the afternoon away

Motor scooters hum by
the cars are few, and sigh
I feel like I could laugh or cry down here
on Love Pavement

My eyes cross the table like wary predators
I see your jacket, see your bag
your cigarettes and fashion mag
its pages idly falling from suit to perfume

Beside your coffee there's a purple stone
and a bunch of keys
a soft caressing summer breeze
and a hand that taps its fingers
holds the spoon and lingers
points at a map, then forwards
to Love Pavement

I follow the line of your attention
The girl opposite, gawky again, laughs
as she buys a shirt for her brother
climbs into her mother's car
We watch it trundle over the cobbles,
tyres popping softly
its shadow stretching towards us as it turns the corner
onto Love Pavement

Love Pavement – slight return no.2

Behind the pavement in a shuttered room
points of light move at the speed
of the sun across the sky.
One touches a sleeping face
and heats it like an invisible flame.
A dream rises through sleeping fog and bursts.
Eyes open, the sleeper winces and awakes;
The dream fragments fall winking in mirror shards
tantalising the memory with
'I wish' and 'maybe'
and 'it's been so long since I saw my baby'
down here on Love Pavement

A ghost ship sails between the houses.
Masts sway, ropes creak
and sailors look into the rooms,
hoping to see more than they ought to,
wisecracks and contraband at the ready.
Curtains swish like sails
and the windows are as blind as
love on the Pavement

Onwards, to the sea a mile away,
can you smell the salt?
The rank mud of the docks sends a heady whiff
into your nose
and you take a sniff
a hint of decay and death
upon the summer's breath
that sidles
down Love Pavement

Cinema over there
next door carpet rolls lean against hot brick.
Plumber, travel agent and bar
and nobody cares who you are

Part of the scenery
no cause for alarm.
Just sitting here I'll come to no harm
and I'll slowly assume the shape...

Three Capital Cities

Washington

Bus, Washington, Sunset

Bus, Washington, Sunset
All aboard, Russians, Japanese, Americans,
Sunset, red, blue, black, international babble,
even German sounds more like home than America

Bus, Washington, Sunset
Passing through low rent, shabby houses,
Gimcrack Edwardiania – Teddy Rooseveldtiana –
Barred windows barred doors broken panels,
Deluxe hair salon 'Grand Opening'
Hand-painted on glass and crooked,
Armoured dry cleaning,
And today's early morning queue outside a liquor store,
Bad neighbourhood.

Bus, Washington, Sunset
Downtown giant scale buildings, no soul or style,
But on Michigan Avenue chain link fences around front yards,
Astro-turf upon porches, neat and weird and acid green.
Capital, Capitol from Penn. Avenue so fucking obvious,
And fuck you, life owes me a living faces, and so on and on...

Bus, Washington, Sunset
Haven't spoken more than ten words to anyone all day,
Listened with half ears though, sometimes more.
Damn those colours are intense beyond belief,
It should be Sri Lanka or Singapore.
It's too hot in here too full, I look out of the window
Darkness falls around me and fills my heart.

Bus, Washington, Sunset
If they knew what I was thinking I'd be deported.
If they blood-tested me they'd know I was a liar too.
How come the skies are so blue,
The trees so green,
Christmas decorations in every lobby and hall.
There should be snow and reindeer,
There should be Jack Frost on the window-panes
Instead I see
Washington, Sunset, through bus windows
And wonder when I will have my next conversation.
Whether I will ever have a conversation at all…

Bus, Washington, Sunset
And when I close my eyes it's all still there in fragments,
Splinters of view and colour
And the folks who serve are black
And those they serve are white.

Bus, Washington, Sunset
My jet-lagged head is full of molasses
And it wants to fall upon my chest
Have some rest
And sleep until the land of nod is never never….
I see a man walking through the trees,
Transparent, and far from the ground
I see a helicopter in black and white fluttering,
A broken moth across the sky
I see a man lower his binoculars,
And there are no eyes behind
I see no bears
I pull upon thin strings and float down like a barrage balloon,
It is almost voluptuous…

Bus, Washington, Sunset
And each time I pass through that district on the hill
It is the only real place in Washington, America
Because things are broken there
And it could be another London
It could be the real world.

London

From A Window

Red neon, kebab shop, Holloway Road
The glowing conical doner sign, shape of a pint
Sometimes I glitch in my stride
To watch him peel the meat off
With his long, long knife

Framed heads with shoulders attached
Pass smoothly by
Ten feet above the street
Three-quarter profile to me, in obliquity
The susurrus of the bus, lower pitched
Than the murmur of the cars
The whisper of bicycle wheels
The click of high heels.
In their yellow glare,
Plain and unadorned
Passengers head north,
To Finchley perhaps

With the right music and the light off
The view from this multi-pane window
Becomes
A multi-screen movie
Each oblong a scene, a story of its own
Some stories, the ones in the upper night sky
Are slow, and deep, and darkest blue

But nearer to the ground,
The triangle of light between striding legs

Becomes a silhouette
Against the doorway of the launderette
Then I lose his shins, and in a trice, the rest of him
Even when I crane, and eyeball the chippie next door
(Is that a saveloy? Do they still exist?
Is the customer at the counter stoned or pissed?)

Here is the story of the street lamp and the tree
How do they relate? React?
What room does one make in its life for the other?
I'll keep an eye on them both, benignly, like an uncle
Or an older brother
Hoping for news of a third-party romance
The best bits, not the breakup…

And this one is a road movie with
An enigmatic ending, made in California in the 1970s
Almost starring Dennis Hopper,
You know the one
It finishes on the streets of LA, though it doesn't,
Because this is North London

And the tale of the pavement is waiting to claim you
Acne'd with chewing gum, obdurate, hard
Obstinate, objective, and
Distinctly lacking in compassion.
I do not want the pavement as my destination,
Though I have dreamed of the gutter

There's little time between cars to become flotsam
More time to become jetsam
At the Coronet pub, a Wetherspoons
Where you get a free pensioner with every table in the room

But we all know there are worse things
You can do with a day
Than drink cheap beer
When your accumulated years
Are running on fumes.

Holloway Kebab House, formerly
Holloway Best Kebab, formerly
China Buffet, formerly The May Malay...
Back then, under bamboo awnings,
Ripe with dust
And fish so delicious it would make you weep
The story of a man,
Once in foreign service,
Singapore, a sad post-colonial hint
And she's May, and she's Malay, and
She's the cook, the chef, and his wife,
But no one knows why
Times were hard and McDonalds is now on the corner where
A shoe shop once stood,
And the popularity of burgers
Casually killed the May Malay, but hey,
People still got to eat!

I gather the strands greedily,
Orchestrate the narrative
Conduct the pavement promenade
Watch the windows opposite
Hoping for a plot, a motive, a scenario to emerge
Only to find that I'm the one being observed,
I am in someone else's movie
I am an incident in another life
I've been, and stayed, and gone,
Like an epitaph, or a half-remembered song.

Berlin

I Saw Michael Caine

I saw Michael Caine on the underground in Berlin.
He was on his way to work
with a package of sandwiches on his lap.
Of course, it wasn't really Michael Caine,
but this man was his spitting image.
His hair was dark though,
but Michael Caine would have looked like that,
if he had dark hair.
And if he'd been carrying sandwiches
on the underground, in Berlin.

Even, I would like to conjecture,
down to the sandwiches themselves, and perhaps
the very material in which they were wrapped.

You have to think of it this way.
If Michael Caine travelled to work on the U-Bahn
in Berlin,
dark-haired, but definitely wearing the right glasses
what would he use – on a regular basis –
for wrapping his sandwiches in?

I think it would help if we refer to his films,
the really important ones,
the ones that formed our perception of his character.

Alfie - not much sandwich information in that one,
café food and home cooking mostly.

The girl he lived with
would have tried to be modern;
in the historical absence of clingfilm
she would probably have chosen polythene bags,
or something like that.

The Harry Palmer films are more like it though.
The opening sequence of The Ipcress File
is redolent of the careful gourmet.
This man wouldn't use polythene
to cover sandwiches made with good fresh bread.
It would go rubbery in minutes.
Neither would he use aluminium foil –
condensation again, you see.
Someone like Harry Palmer
would almost certainly settle for
greaseproof paper.
I'm sure of it.
He loved pure flavours, and
greaseproof paper
doesn't change the flavour of its content.
As long as it wasn't for long-term sandwich storage,
Harry Palmer would have used
greaseproof paper.

Now, Michael Caine himself has a reputation
as a bit of a gastronome.
He has invested in restaurants, and that sort of thing.
One can safely assume he would be pretty demanding
of whatever he wrapped his sandwiches in.
So that's it.

Couldn't be anything else
when you think about it logically.

If Michael Caine travelled to work on the Berlin underground, he would DEFINITELY have his sandwiches wrapped in greaseproof paper!

Get Carter was pretty good too.
More of a steak and chips than a sandwich movie though.

Three Hampshire Pubs

Dusty Springfield (The Anchor, Basingstoke)

Walking on a Summer evening past an open window
Meal being eaten, cutlery overheard
A 'clink'
Like a penny in a great big bottle
In a pub
In a street
In a town where I once lived

Change from my drink
Dropped down the neck for charity
Then glancing at the Jukebox
Dusty's 'Goin' Back'
Last coin gone,
I shrug
Finish my half, and turn to leave.
Pub door swings slowly on creaking springs,
And as I walk out, the first bars,
Then Dusty sings

I hold the door, and see you standing
Hair shadowing your face, over the Wurlitzer
I waver, I wonder
Who's playing our song?
When I don't even know you yet.

Usually too shy, I step in
And move at the song's slow rhythm
Dusty gives me courage
While singing of its lack
I speak, you speak, you smile, we talk until
Closing time,

And you didn't mind
Paying for the drinks, or the bus home
Where we kissed
On the back seat, of course

And the next day, you went back
To Scotland.

Not Being Bored (The Purefoy, Preston Candover)

When ennui bites or pain ignites,
I immerse myself in the memory of a time and space,
A summer evening, a special place,
A 1960's tennis club in a Hampshire farming village,
Neither shabby nor aching with privilege.

I dream of folded hills and beech hangers,
Pigeons on a summer's eve,
Calling for their supper,
Their voices make murmurous mutter
Then sudden silence as a trotting fox approaches.
Keep Schtum for Reynard,
He won't see us, soon he'll move to town,
He'll find the way along the railway track.
In a few years' time he'll be high on KFC and smoking crack.

And here is a shattered snail shell,
Remnants of a thrush's snack,
Or the hurried breakfast of a rat.
But in this copse of majestic trees lurks a corpse,
A rabbit waiting for maggots,
It's myxy tainted flesh too rank
For scavengers' teeth, or knives and forks
.
The dappling light of evening sun,
Shafts of the golden hour spangling,
It's a glorious beauty if you ignore the smell,
The rotten whiff from hell,
That inspires gut wrenching heaves
Beneath luminous green leaves.

So, I float back to the comforting muted thwack
Of Slazenger racquet on scuffed white ball,
Of a game that lasts till the sun has gone
And ends too close to call

Twilight obscures the court
And later, in the car, outside the pub
Orange squash and crisps that my mother bought
To appease us while inside, she drank her gin and tonic
And sometimes I wonder
If any of it happened at all.

The Plough at Lunchtime (East Stratton)

After the raucous middle-aged crowd
and their Border terriers departed,
a swiftly flowing flood of wealthy Aryan children
took over the big table by the window.
They were nearly all blonde,
not a true brunette amongst them.
Three little boys, four little girls,
several as cute as catalogue kids,
all attractive in that clear-skinned, nannied way.

There was a Hugo, naturally,
who shot intelligent arrogant conversational arrows at his father.
Daddy up by the bar,
laying into the commercialisation of Christmas.
"So ghastly, the religious significance of the holiday forgotten
in the greedy rush of consumerism."

"It doesn't mean anything anymore, just a sham,
a façade for shopkeepers, and for children.
There's nothing you or I can do about it,
the sense of ceremony, the importance of the birth of Christ...
Just a pack of little devils tearing open a heap of gifts
without even stopping to see what they've received,
or who it came from!"

"Can I have a lemonade please, my darling Daddy?"
Asked the cutest girl of all.
I nearly screamed,
I nearly cried.

Three Holidays

France

Vieux Ruffec

Greening of singed hearts
beneath the leaves of summer,
in this vegetable remembrance I sing.
Few words and whispers left,
as sated flesh we lay
in tangled white,
and night-blown ravished sleep.

Fresh smoke arose from dawn,
and sunward spiralled,
butter for the soul,
perfume of toast and wine.
My larcenous heart wanted to steal it all for us,
steal it all away

Spain

Bull Dancing

If I should go to Spain again
Will I thrill to Flamenco fighting?
Or move like olive-oiled lightning, prancing
With sheer delight to see bull dancing?

Down at the harbour the pigeons
Toss breadcrumbs to the cooing biddies
One waddles with a limp,
He should walk with a stick
Spin it on his wing with a practiced flick
Life is grand on this side of the fountain

Flashing teeth and smiling knives
Toledo steals and shortens lives
It's much macho on the shore where
Muscle boys float by
Moored to less as they try to guess
Who and where and why

The victims of their ignorance
Sometimes kiss
And sometimes cry

UK

Brighton Rocks

Brighton rocks under zero stress
See the young blades' stiletto flash
Distract the roamers
And home sweet homers

The beach, the prom with a crippled lift
A Betjeman station under steel construction kit
Protected with prophylactic certainty
Like the cellophane masks upon the snacks
While just yards away
Burgers taint the sea air

Maybe I'll see her, once more single
As the pink bodies
Freeze in a blink
Motionless, shimmering on the salty shingle

Three for Winter

The Swan

On the way to lunch we passed a dead swan.
We were looking at the unusual number of buzzards
standing calmly on the fences and verges,
dreaming of road-kill.
Our quiet Mercedes left their table bare.
The fields were flat and frozen,
with ice-filled furrows leading in lines towards the wooded ridge
that rose to our left.
To the right,
a suspicion of mountains lurked
behind the seemingly eternal winter mists
of northern Germany.

There were four or five swans in the middle of one field,
and the tattered white flag of surrendered life in another nearby.
"They are starving," said Helmut,
"The rivers are frozen, and the ground. This winter is too cold."
I realise that the buzzards have in fact fled the mountains
for the comparative warmth of the flatlands.
Our Sunday peace is made melancholy
by the struggle for life.

We move smoothly forwards, through villages, past farms,
and I wonder if the birds know they are dying,
or feel the gnawing hunger.
There was no expression on their faces,
as far as I could glimpse,
no hint of anthropomorphic Disney grimaces, or tears.
Nature's reality in the numb, chilled fields
is as harsh as the landscape,
as inelegant as the broken bird beside its' still living family,
and as beautiful as all of that too.

We turn onto a typically poplar lined main road
that cut across the valley with impersonal directness.
A very small part of me stays with the swans,
under the watchful scrutiny of the buzzards.
I mourn without emotion,
not bothering to guard the corpse from beaks and talons.
The buzzards cannot be denied their chance
of surviving the winter
on the misfortunes of others.

At lunch I eat too many onions
I feel a twinge of guilt and indigestion
as we pass the swans again upon our return.
My pain is from eating,
Theirs, from not
Serves me right

White Bull

A white bull planted four-square
Each leg an inverted oak tree of flesh, sinew, bone
Steaming in the soft grey rain

Vapour poured from his nostrils
Twin jets of a silent engine
Whistling

Huge flanks, coiffed curly poll
Still steaming
In the soft grey rain

One Day, One Night

Day

As dawn broke we came down from the mountains
Cruising in near silence through the crystal air
Light spilled
Dregs from an upturned cup
Seeping across the estuary like a slow benign stain

We swept over the causeway and sliced the bay in two
One side still in darkness behind the high stone wall
The other, the dawn of time

A single peak raised itself on high
Greenness flowed down its flanks
Changing dark mysteries into forests
And grey wasteland into frosted meadows
I slowed down and opened the window

Smelling salt and dew
And the hint of a cigar from an hour ago

I suddenly remember you are beside me

Night

I was up there in a blizzard once
Headlights flailing the darkness
My heart in my mouth
The road dipped and swooped away from me
Rising up in alarm before the elemental onslaught

I jinked left to avoid a snow-grazing sheep
Wobbled dangerously close to a ragged barbed wire fence
And recovering flicked off the stereo
I needed to hear myself think

My heartbeat slowed
And I wanted to stop
And let the snow cover the car in a protective skin
I would drift into exposure and die beautifully in my sleep

I drove carefully onward into the orange streetlights of Ffestiniog
The last wet flakes melted on the windscreen
As I reached the coast

Three at Random

The Radio Shop

Not just radios, but refrigerators, stereos,
electric and Spanish guitars,
snare drum, sticks, stands and straps.
Switches wires cables bulbs sockets toasters,
and electric frying pans coveted by the plastic rain-hooded women
who descend in a covey upon the counter.

"Can't afford the top model but the cheaper one has dust on the box
Tut tut, means they don't sell so well…"

"No no, it's just a dusty shop, it gets like that in a week I swear.
Mrs Williams bought one just like it,
 and it was a boon to her, a boon."

"Aunty Iris wanted one
oh, it would have saved lighting that old stove
so early in the morning
an extra half an hour in bed with a cuppa
I gave her an electric kettle for Christmas
let me see seven years ago it must be, or was it eight?"
"No seven cos that's when I had the operation isn't that so?"

"Yes, the lid comes with it
and you can do stew in it at a pinch."

"I ought to buy it for Aunty Iris
but I'm not sure she'd appreciate it as much as me
how much is it now?
Well that's not too bad is it and what do you think?"
"Well I don't know it looks very nice
but how often would she use it?"

"Never can tell with Ron and the boys
and soon there'll be grandchildren or my name isn't…"
"Oh, go on you might as well,
money doesn't spend itself you know."

"Shall I wrap it up?"
"Yes please, and here's the money."
"Here's the change and a good day to you.
The plug is included."

Flight

A flock of aeroplanes materialises over La Cienega Boulevard,
all shapes and sizes, of every aviatic era.
As suddenly as they appear they begin to fall,
fuel-less, helpless.
A Spitfire tumbles into an antique shop,
a Comet crunches into the roof of the Beverly Centre.
We sit tight in the car,
bewildered but not particularly frightened.
Every mechanical object,
every machine has come to a halt.

As the airplanes smash and crash around us out of a clear blue sky
we act like train-spotters in a railway heaven.
"Look! A DH4!"
"A Spad!"
"A Grumman Wildcat!"
"A Heinkel bomber!"
No injuries appear to be sustained.
We look in vain for pilots but the wreckage is free of human life.
These remnants of a Bermuda triangle are strangely benign.

A group of teenagers laugh
as they dodge the fatally folding wings of a Lysander.
The bi-planes spin and drop like sycamore seeds,
propellers propelling only themselves,
clattering on the blacktop.

Jets pierce the pavements and stand near vertical,
quivering momentarily
as their descent ends with cartoon abruptness.

A Phantom whines like a Mosquito,
a Mosquito thrums like a cockchafer,
both collide in pretty splinters just above our heads.
Slivers of broken fuselage rain down upon us,
some falling onto the back seat of our convertible.

The lights change, and the cars cough back into life.
The traffic resumes,
and rubber-necking drivers
dodgem into each other with surprise.

A darkening above us recedes, as a Zeppelin,
seconds from destruction but a moment ago,
now rises in diminishing perspective
until it is smaller than a gull flying over the Hollywood Hills.

Last September

My head rests in clouds of wild Marjoram
I can see the stars at last,

And moonlight sifting through the trees
Paints the cornfields
Night, white, moleskin, velvet.

It's too beautiful to be spoiled
Taste of the moon
Scent of herbs and
Earth warm beneath

The frozen light batheing us
Clean slates

Other Excellent Titles from London Poetry Books

londonpoetrybooks.com

There is a Tune	*Cathy Flower*
Dark Matter	*Amy Smith*
Pathways	*Anne Gaelan*
The Mirrors of Thespis	
Pocket full of Whispers	
Kissed by Honey Bees	*Keith Robert Bray*
Counteroffensive	*Steve Tasane*
English is a Foreign Language	
Outside In, musing on life as an Autistic Poet	*Alain English*
Ooetry	*Wendy Young*
Death Suicide Despair Poetry	
Life and Hope	*Jason Harris*
In the Name of the Flesh	*Ernesto Sarezale*
The Bird of Morning	
Of the Deep	*IDF. Andrew*
Twisted and Chewed 2	*Shaun Rivers*
Tomorrow We Fight	
Yesterday's Men	*Lizzie Rose*
Everybody is a Diagnosis	*Richard Allan*
Running Through Trees and Glitter	*Rachel Tansy Chadwick*
My Inside Opened Up	*Patricia Flowers*